What Was Cooking in Martha Washington's Presidential Mansions?

Tanya Larkin

The Rosen Publishing Group's
PowerKids Press™
New York

The recipes in this cookbook are intended for a child to make together with an adult.

Many thanks to Ruth Rosen and her test kitchen.

Published in 2001 by The Rosen Publishing Group, Inc.
29 East 21st Street, New York, NY 10010

First Edition

Book Design: Danielle Primiceri
Layout Design: Maria E. Melendez

Photo Credits: pp. 4, 21 © Bettman/CORBIS; pp. 7, 9, 13, 19 by Thaddeus Harden; pp. 10, 14, 17 © SuperStock.

Larkin, Tanya.
    What was cooking in Martha Washington's presidential mansions? / Tanya Larkin.—1st ed.
      p. cm.— (Cooking throughout American history)
    Includes index.
    Summary: Describes Martha Washington, wife of the first president of the United States, her activities during the Revolutionary War and as first lady, and some of the food she served at various stages in her life. Includes recipes.
    ISBN 0-8239-5606-7 (alk. paper)
    1. Cookery, American—Juvenile literature. 2. Washington, Martha, 1731-1802—Juvenile literature. [1. Washington, Martha, 1731-1802. 2. First ladies. 3. Women—Biography. 4. Cookery, American.] I. Title. II. Series.

TX715.L31826 2000
641.3'00973'09033—dc21   00-039168

Manufactured in the United States of America

Contents

The First Lady

Martha Washington was the wife of George Washington, the first president of the United States. The president's wife is known as the first lady, so Martha Washington was the nation's first first lady. People called her "Lady Washington."

George Washington was president for two **terms**, from 1789 to 1797. While George was president, Martha had many responsibilities as the first lady. The Washingtons **hosted** many state dinners for government **officials** and visiting **dignitaries**.

Martha welcomed guests to the presidential home. She oversaw nearly all the meals served to her family and their guests. She was also famous for her cake recipes. Visitors were impressed by the first lady's warm personality and delicious cooking.

◀ *This painting shows George and Martha Washington with Martha's children, Patsy and Jack, from her first marriage.*

George and Martha at Mount Vernon

George Washington was not yet president when he married Martha Custis on January 6, 1759. He and Martha lived at Mount Vernon, George's **plantation** in Virginia. About 300 people worked there, including many **slaves**. Later, George and others of his time would reject the terrible practice of slavery.

Even before he became president, George was an important leader in colonial America. George was a general in the army. Many people came to visit George at Mount Vernon. Martha was in charge of the household. Slaves who worked in Martha's kitchen helped her prepare for the many visitors. The Mount Vernon kitchen did not have stoves or refrigerators. Food was cooked in a fireplace that was so big you could stand up in it. One of the foods cooked in the fireplace was Indian hoe cakes, one of George's favorite breakfast foods. Hoe cakes got their name because they were once cooked on **hoes** placed in a fire.

Cornbread

¾ cup (177 ml) cornmeal
1 cup (237 ml) flour
⅓ cup (80 ml) sugar
3 teaspoons (15 ml)
    baking powder
¾ teaspoon (4 ml) salt
1 cup (237 ml) milk
1 egg, well beaten
2 tablespoons (30 ml)
    melted shortening
    (butter, margarine, or
    oil)

HOW TO DO IT:

☞ Preheat oven to 425° F (218° C).

☞ Sift the dry ingredients into a bowl: cornmeal, flour, sugar, baking powder, and salt.

☞ Add milk, egg, and shortening.

☞ Mix together.

☞ Pour into a greased, shallow baking dish

☞ Bake for 20 minutes until golden brown.

☞ Cut into wedges and serve warm with butter, honey, or jam. Serves eight.

Cornbread is a delicious substitute that you can make instead of Indian Hoe Cakes. Martha and George also drank "liberty tea," made of dried raspberry leaves and hot water, every morning. They drank this to protest the tea that was sent to the **colonies** from England and was taxed by the king of England.

Martha Brings the Soldiers Food

The American Revolutionary War (1775–1783) interrupted the Washingtons' peaceful life at Mount Vernon. The war was fought by **colonists** who wanted to be free from England's rule. As the commander in chief of the Continental Army, George had to leave Mount Vernon. He was away for more than six of the eight years of the war.

During the war, George and his soldiers were in many camps in different **colonies**. Martha visited George every winter. In the winter of 1778, Martha bravely made her way to Valley Forge, Pennsylvania, to visit George and his soldiers. She found them starving and cold. Martha made bandages and helped take care of wounded soldiers. She also tried to cheer up the soldiers by bringing them her special fruitcake with candied cherries.

Cherry Bread Pudding

You will need:

12 thickly cut slices of bread

6-8 tablespoons (90-120 ml) butter

1 cup (237 ml) cherry preserves

½ teaspoon (2.5 ml) grated nutmeg

3 teaspoons (15 ml) lemon peel, grated

3 cups (710 ml) whole milk

4 eggs, slightly beaten

⅓ cup (80 ml) sugar

HOW TO DO IT:

☞ Preheat oven to 325° F (165° C)

☞ Grease the bottom and sides of a baking dish.

☞ Spread bread thickly with butter. Trim crusts.

☞ Cover the bottom of the baking dish with slices of bread, buttered side facing up.

☞ Spread a layer of cherry preserves over the bread.

☞ Sprinkle some of the nutmeg and lemon peel over the layer of cherry preserves.

☞ Repeat the last three steps, stacking layers of bread, cherry preserves, nutmeg, and lemon peel, until the dish is full. Set aside.

☞ Mix together milk, eggs, and sugar in a mixing bowl.

☞ Pour the mixture over the bread layers.

☞ Allow the bread to soak up the liquid.

☞ Bake in oven for one hour or until lightly browned.

☞ Slice and serve warm. Serves six.

George and Martha Move to New York City

The Continental Army, led by George Washington, won the war against the British in 1783. George and Martha went back to their peaceful life in Mount Vernon, but not for long. In 1789, George was elected the country's first president. At that time, there was no White House. The first presidential home was at 10 Cherry Street in New York City. George and Martha moved to New York City to take up their roles as the president and first lady. It was suggested that they **rotate** invitations for inviting guests. The system of rotating guest lists helped people get their turn as guests of the new president and first lady. Every Tuesday afternoon, George hosted an informal **reception**. George and Martha hosted **formal** dinner parties together on Thursday evenings.

◀ *George and Martha entertained guests almost every day at the presidential mansion in New York City. Many people wanted to be invited to the president's home.*

A Charming Hostess

On Fridays Martha hosted a reception. Martha's Friday afternoon reception was sometimes called a "drawing room," since it took place in the mansion's drawing room, or parlor. Martha usually served plum cake, lemonade, tea, and coffee to a group of ladies. Abigail Adams, the wife of vice president John Adams, was often among the guests. Abigail once commented that Martha served food at these receptions in a very nice and tasteful way.

Martha was always a charming **hostess**, but she had to look out for George's well-being. At exactly 9:00 in the evening, Martha would open the window to let their dinner guests know that it was time for them to go home. Martha wanted to make sure that the president got a full night's sleep.

Lemonade

2 cups (473 ml) sugar
1 cup (237 ml) water
6 lemons (or enough
    lemons to make 1 cup
    (237 ml) lemon juice
ice water

HOW TO DO IT:

☞ Place the sugar and water in a saucepan.

☞ Have an adult help you heat the sugar-water mixture until it boils. Boil for five minutes.

☞ The mixture will become a syrup.

☞ After five minutes, have an adult remove the pan from the heat. Then cool thoroughly.

☞ Strain the fresh lemon juice to remove pulp.

☞ Add the lemon juice to the syrup. This makes it a lemon syrup.

☞ Add two tablespoons (30 ml) of the lemon syrup to a glass of ice water.

☞ Stir and enjoy.

☞ Refrigerate any leftover lemon syrup in a covered jar.

Sundays With the Children

Martha Washington worked hard at being a good first lady. As time went on, she became more comfortable in the role. It also helped that she had one day a week out of the spotlight. Martha took a break from her duties as first lady on Sundays. On Sundays, the Washingtons did not entertain guests. They spent the day with their family. George and Martha did not have any children together, but Martha had two children, Patsy and Jack, from an earlier marriage. Martha's first husband had died. The Washingtons loved children. They enjoyed giving ice cream and cake parties on Saturday afternoons. President Washington would send his own carriage to pick up the young guests. Fraunces was the cook at the presidential home in New York City. He made delicious cake, candy, and ice cream for the children's parties.

◀ *George and Martha Washington enjoyed Sundays with their family.*

Another Home in New York City

In 1790, on George's 58th birthday, the Washingtons moved to another presidential home in New York City. This mansion, called Macomb's, was on a street called Broadway. The Washingtons paid $1,000 a year to live at Macomb's. This money came out of the president's $25,000 salary.

The new dining room could seat 20 guests. This meant that that Washingtons could hold even larger state dinners. As always, Martha made sure to follow proper **etiquette**. Formal dinner parties began at 4:00 in the afternoon. Guests were expected to be on time. At these dinners, Martha sat on one side of the table with the women guests on either side of her. George sat across from Martha with the gentlemen guests on either side of him.

Martha Washington was the hostess for many parties. ▶

A Dinner Party

In 1790, the capital of the nation was moved from New York City to Philadelphia. George and Martha Washington never lived in the White House that presidents live in today. The White House was not built until 1800. In Philadelphia the president and first lady lived in the Morris House at 190 High Street.

The Morris House had a lovely, walled garden with fruit trees. Changes were made to make the house more comfortable for the president and first lady. For example, the dining room's **bow windows** were made larger so that the room would hold more guests. The menu for a typical dinner party might have included soup, fish, chicken, turkey, and different kinds of meat for the main course. Dessert would begin with apple pies, puddings, ice creams, and jellies. The meals ended with melons, baked apples, peaches and other fruits that were in season, and nuts.

Baked Apples

You will need:

6 large, firm apples
(Granny Smith, Empire)
6 teaspoons (30 ml) butter
or margarine
½ cup (118 ml) brown
sugar
¼ cup (59 ml) raisins
¼ cup chopped (59 ml)
walnuts (optional)
½ cup (118 ml) heavy
cream (optional)
water

HOW TO DO IT:

☞ Preheat oven to 350° F (177° C)

☞ Wash and dry apples.

☞ Have an adult help cut out the cores of the apples.

☞ Place apples in a baking dish with the tops up.

☞ Fill each core with two teaspoons (10 ml) of brown
sugar.

☞ Add one teaspoon (five ml) each of raisins and
walnuts (optional) into center of each apple .

☞ Pour enough water in the dish to cover 1/3 of the
apples.

☞ Have an adult place pan with apples in preheated
oven.

☞ Bake until apples can be easily pierced with a fork.

☞ Have an adult remove the pan. Let cool.

☞ You may serve with heavy cream. Serves six.

The First Lady in Philadelphia

Martha was used to being the first lady by the time she moved to Philadelphia. She was used to having lots of people around who wanted her attention. She began to enjoy being the first lady. Martha and George continued to give parties in Philadelphia, but they began to go to more parties, too. It was nice for Martha to be a guest instead of the hostess.

George Washington's first term ended in 1793, but he agreed to serve a second term. His decision upset Martha greatly. Although she enjoyed being the first lady, she also looked forward to returning to the peace and privacy of Mount Vernon. She loved George and wanted to support him, so she agreed to stay with him in Philadelphia while he served his second term.

This painting shows Martha Washington as a young woman. ▶

Return to Mount Vernon

Two weeks after George Washington turned 65, he was given a birthday party by the city of Philadelphia. The party was also a farewell party for him and Martha. George's presidency was almost over. George and Martha would be going home to Mount Vernon. Martha wore a beautiful orange satin gown to the party. Once at home in Mount Vernon, the Washingtons continued to receive guests. One night during dinner, George turned to Martha and remarked that it was the first time they were dining alone in 20 years! In 1799, George Washington died after a brief illness. In his **will** he released half of the slaves that he had owned. Martha released the rest of the slaves the following year. Martha missed George dearly. Her granddaughter Nelly helped to take care of Martha for many years. Martha died in 1802. She was buried next to her husband at Mount Vernon.

Glossary

bow windows (BOH WIN-doz) Windows that are built on a curve and jut out from a wall.

colonies (KAH-luh-neez) An area in a new country where a large group of people move, who are still ruled by the leaders and laws of their old country.

colonists (KAH-luh-nists) People who live in a colony.

dignitaries (DIG-nuh-ter-eez) People who hold important positions in the government.

etiquette (EH-tih-kit) The polite and proper way of doing something. The usual rules for behavior.

formal (FOR-mel) According to set rules.

hoes (HOZ) A tool with a thin, flat blade at the end of a long stick. Used for weeding a garden.

hosted (HOST-ed) To have entertained guests.

hostess (HOST-ess) A person who gives a party and invites guests.

officials (U-fih-shulz) People who hold public office.

plantation (plan-TAY-shun) A very large farm where crops like tobacco and cotton were grown. Many plantation owners used slaves to work these farms.

reception (rih-SEP-shun) A large formal gathering for meeting people.

rotate (ROH-tate) To change a fixed order.

slaves (SLAYVZ) People who are "owned" by another person and are forced to work for him or her.

terms (TURMZ) Specific periods of time that an elected official can serve.

will (WIL) A legal document describing how a person's property will be given away or managed after that person's death.

Index

Web Sites

To learn more about Martha and George Washington, check out these Web sites:

http://www.whitehouse.gov/WH/glimpse/presidents/html/gov1.html
http://www.education-world.com/a_lesson051.shtml